D1524650

by Joanne Mattern

New Hanover County Public Library
201 Chestnut Street
Wilmington. North Carolina 28401

CAPSTONE PRESS
a capstone imprint

Edge Books are published by Capstone Press,
151 Good Counsel Drive, P.O. Box 669, Mankato, Minnesota 56002.
www.capstonepub.com

Copyright © 2011 by Capstone Press, a Capstone imprint.
All rights reserved.
No part of this publication may be reproduced in whole or in part,
or stored in a retrieval system, or transmitted in any form or by any means,
electronic, mechanical, photocopying, recording, or otherwise, without
written permission of the publisher.
For information regarding permission, write to Capstone Press,
151 Good Counsel Drive, P.O. Box 669, Dept. R, Mankato, Minnesota 56002.

Books published by Capstone Press are manufactured with paper
containing at least 10 percent post-consumer waste.

Library of Congress Cataloging-in-Publication Data
Mattern, Joanne, 1963–
 Birman cats.
   p. cm.—(Edge books. All about cats)
 Includes bibliographical references and index.
 Summary: "Describes the history, physical features, temperament, and care of
   the Birman cat breed"—Provided by publisher.
 ISBN 978-1-4296-6629-9 (library binding)
 1. Birman cat—Juvenile literature. I. Title. II. Series.
 SF449.B5M373 2011
 636.8'24—dc22   2010037114

Editorial Credits
Leah K. Pockrandt and Carrie Braulick Sheely, editors; Heidi Thompson,
   designer; Wanda Winch, media researcher; Eric Manske,
   production specialist

Photo Credits
Alamy: David Hosking, 6, David Kilpatrick, 25, directphoto.bz, 27, tbkmedia.
de, 9; Courtesy of the Kittkat Cattery, Coventry, R.I., 13; Getty Images: Dorling
Kindersley/David King, 10, Steve Lyne, 21, 23, 29; iStockphoto: Cagri Özgür, 5;
Ron Kimball Stock/Alan Robinson, 15; Shutterstock: Eric Isselée, cover, Linn
Currie, 17, 18, 20

Printed in the United States of America in Stevens Point, Wisconsin.
062011   006228WZVMI

TABLE OF CONTENTS

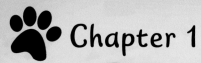

Chapter 1

TREASURED BEAUTIES

Birman cats are known as the "sacred cats of Burma." Birmans got this nickname because the cats may have once lived in temples with Birman priests. The priests are thought to have treasured the good-natured cats as loyal pets.

Modern Birman owners also treasure their cats. Many people like Birmans because they are calm and affectionate. People also value the breed's unique look. Long fur, bold **colorpoints**, and pure white paws set the Birman apart from other breeds.

In 2009 the Birman was the ninth most popular breed in the Cat Fanciers' Association (CFA). It was also one of the five most popular longhaired breeds. The CFA is the world's largest cat **registry**.

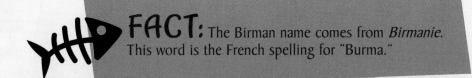

FACT: The Birman name comes from *Birmanie*. This word is the French spelling for "Burma."

colorpoint—a pattern in which the ears, face, tail, and legs are darker than the base color

registry—an organization that keeps track of the ancestry for cats of a certain breed

The Birman's pure white paws make it unique from other breeds with colorpoints.

FACT: Most U.S. Birman breeders follow a French tradition of naming their cats. They give all kittens born in the same year names that begin with the same letter.

By buying a Birman kitten from a breeder, you can often see what the kitten's parents look like.

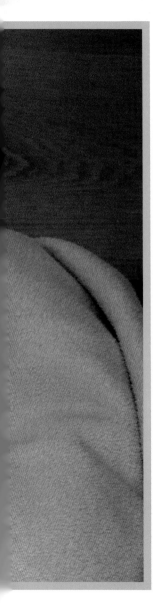

IS THE BIRMAN RIGHT FOR YOU?

Birmans make good family pets. These friendly, gentle cats seem to enjoy being around people and other animals. Birmans get along well with dogs and most other cats. They do not seem to like being alone. Owners should have other pets in the house if no people are at home during the day.

Birmans generally have few health problems and are easy to care for. Even though Birmans have long hair, the hair does not mat easily.

You can find a Birman in one of several ways. Visiting a breeder is one of the best ways to find a Birman. Responsible breeders carefully select their cats for breeding. They make sure that the cats are healthy.

You may be able to find a Birman through a breed rescue organization or an animal shelter. These organizations help find new, loving homes for pets. Some Birmans from breed rescue organizations might even be registered with the CFA or another registry.

Chapter 2

BIRMAN HISTORY

No clear record of the Birman's origin exists. But there is one popular story that describes how the Birman got its coloring. A priest named Mun-Ha lived in the temple of Lao-Tsun. People worshiped a blue-eyed goddess named Tsun-Kyan-Kse at this temple. White longhaired cats with yellow eyes helped guard the temple. The temple's head priest, Mun-Ha, had a cat named Sihn.

One day thieves attacked the temple. They killed Mun-Ha in front of a golden statue of Tsun-Kyan-Kse. Sihn placed his feet on his master and faced the golden statue. Sihn's white fur then took on a golden glow. His face, ears, legs, and tail turned dark brown to match the earth. But Sihn's paws turned white where they touched Mun-Ha's head. Sihn's eyes also turned from yellow to dark blue.

The legend says that Mun-Ha's soul left his body and entered Sihn. The cat stayed by his dead master's body for seven days before he also died.

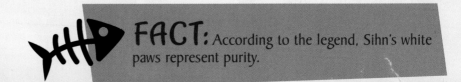

FACT: According to the legend, Sihn's white paws represent purity.

A legend explains how the Birman got its blue eyes and the golden mist on its coat.

Some people believed Sihn carried Mun-Ha's soul to heaven when he died. After Sihn's death, the coats and eye color of the other cats in the temple changed in the same way. The legend says that each cat carries the soul of a priest on his journey to the afterlife.

The golden mist of Birmans ranges in shade. Cats with very dark colorpoints often have a deep golden glow.

MORE MYSTERIES

The origin of the first Birman cats in Europe is as mysterious as the origin of the breed. No one is really sure when the first Birman cats came to Europe. One story says that two Englishmen helped Burmese priests protect their temple during World War I (1914–1918). The men were Major Gordon Russell and August Pavie. To show their thanks, the priests sent a pair of Birmans to the men while they were living in France.

Another story says that a wealthy American received a pair of Birman cats from a temple servant in Burma. The man's full name is not known, but the story says his last name was Vanderbilt. Mr. Vanderbilt then sent the cats to a friend in France.

BEYOND THE STORIES

While many stories exist, there are a few generally accepted facts about the Birman's history in Europe. Someone in Burma sent a pair of Birman cats to another person in France in 1919. The male Birman was named Maldapour. The female cat was named Sita. Maldapour did not survive the long journey. But Sita gave birth to kittens when she arrived in France.

One kitten was named Poupee. Many people believe Poupee was bred to a Siamese cat. Siamese cats have colorpoints like Birmans do. In 1925 French cat associations recognized Birmans.

The Birman breed almost died out in Europe during World War II (1939–1945). Many people believe only two Birmans were alive at the end of the war. These cats were bred to Persians and cats of other breeds. This crossbreeding allowed the Birman traits to continue. Even though these Birmans were crossbred, people still considered them to be Birmans.

BIRMANS IN THE UNITED STATES

The first Birman cats probably arrived in the United States in 1959. In 1961 cat breeder Gertrude Griswold received two colorpointed cats as a gift. She later discovered that the cats were Birmans. She arranged to breed these cats with Birmans from France. Griswold's breeding program helped build interest in Birman cats in the United States.

FACT: A Birman first received a CFA National Winner title in the 1988–1989 show season. National Winner titles are given to the highest scoring cats of a show season.

Other North American breeders soon bought Birmans from breeders in England and France. In 1967 the CFA recognized the breed. Five years later, a cat named Griswold's Romar of Bybee became the first Birman to win a CFA Grand Champion title. Over time the Birman breed gained popularity in North America.

Owners make sure their Birmans are clean and expertly groomed for shows.

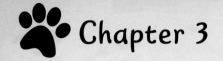

Chapter 3

GLOVES AND LACES

Birmans are medium-sized cats. Males can weigh as much as 14 pounds (6.4 kilograms). Females can weigh up to 11 pounds (5 kg). A Birman's long body is sturdy and muscular. Birmans have thick legs, round paws, and a medium-length tail.

COLORS

Birman cats have four traditional coat colors. These colors are seal point, blue point, chocolate point, and lilac point. The four colors are called traditional because they naturally occur in the breed. Seal-point Birmans have ivory coats with dark brown points. The points on some seal-point Birmans look almost black.

Chocolate-point Birmans have ivory coats with light brown points. Dark blue-gray points mark blue points. These cats have blue-white to pale ivory coats. Lilac points have off-white coats and light pink-gray points.

In the CFA, the ideal Birman coat color has a slight golden tone. The misty golden color often appears on a cat's sides and back.

FACT: Birmans may take three years to fully develop. Many other cat breeds are fully grown after one year.

a lilac-point Birman (bottom) and a blue-point Birman (top)

Some breeders have mated Birmans to cats of other breeds. This crossbreeding has produced colors other than the traditional ones. Today's Birmans can have a variety of colors and patterns. Lynx-point cats have lightly striped coats and more heavily striped points. Other Birmans have cream bodies and deep red points. Tortie-point Birmans have brown points with a mix of another color such as red or cream.

WHAT CAUSES COLORPOINTS?

Colorpoints are produced by a **gene** in Birman cats. This special gene is heat sensitive. Cool parts of the Birman body have dark fur. These body parts include the ears, tail, and face. Warm parts of the Birman body have lighter-colored fur. Birman kittens are born white. Their points begin to appear when they are a few days old. Dark-colored Birmans such as seal points often develop their colorpoints earlier than light-colored Birmans do.

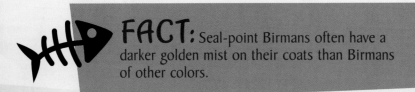

FACT: Seal-point Birmans often have a darker golden mist on their coats than Birmans of other colors.

gene—a part of every cell that carries physical and behavioral information passed from parents to their offspring

a tortie-point Birman

17

A Birman with gloves that extend evenly across all four paws
is likely to receive high scores at cat shows.

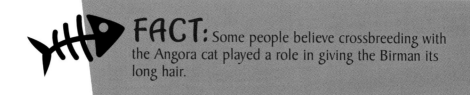

FACT: Some people believe crossbreeding with the Angora cat played a role in giving the Birman its long hair.

MARKINGS

One of a Birman's most noticeable features is its white paw markings, or gloves. The gloves on the back feet extend up the back of the legs. These markings are called laces.

In the CFA, Birmans' gloves and laces should look a certain way for competition. The gloves should stretch across each paw in an even line. The laces should end in a point on the back of the cats' legs. Laces should also line up evenly. It is rare for a Birman to have ideal gloves and laces on all four feet.

COATS

The Birman's thick, long coat is silky to the touch. Many Birmans have a heavy **ruff** and slightly curly hair on their stomachs.

ruff—a fringe or frill of long hairs growing around an animal's neck

19

A Birman's blue eyes are almost perfectly round.

FACIAL FEATURES

Birmans have wide, round heads with a slight flat spot in front of the ears. The ears are set wide apart and are slightly rounded at the tips. The Birman's chin is well developed and its cheeks are full.

A Birman's blue eyes are also wide set. The eye color shade varies. In show cats, the CFA prefers a deep, bright blue color.

PERSONALITY

Many people think the Birman is an ideal companion. Birmans are not as active as some shorthaired breeds or as inactive as some other longhaired breeds.

Birmans usually are very calm. They often quietly watch the activities of people and other animals without interrupting. Because of these actions, many people describe the Birman as a polite cat.

Birman kittens are often more playful than adults.

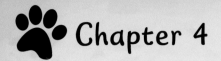

Chapter 4

CARING FOR A BIRMAN

Birmans are strong, healthy cats. With good care, it is common for a Birman to live 15 years or more.

Keeping your Birman indoors is one of the most important things you can do to keep it safe. Cats that roam outdoors face dangers from cars and other animals. These cats also are more likely to become sick.

FEEDING

Like all cats, Birmans need nutritious, balanced diets. Many high-quality pet foods are available in pet stores and supermarkets.

You can feed your cat dry or moist food. Dry food has several advantages. It usually is less expensive than other types of food. Dry food can also help keep cats' teeth clean. It will not spoil if it is left in a dish. Moist food can spoil, so it should not be left out for more than one hour.

Water is a very important part of your cat's diet. Always have a bowl of fresh, clean water available for your Birman.

Kittens may need more food than adult cats because of their increased activity levels.

23

LITTER BOXES

Your cat will need a litter box. This box provides a place for your cat to get rid of bodily waste. The box is filled with small bits of absorbent material called litter. Most cat litter is made of clay, but it can also be made of wood, corn, or other materials.

Cats are clean animals, and they may refuse to use a dirty litter box. Be sure to clean out the box every day. Replace the litter about every two weeks or whenever it appears wet or lumpy.

SCRATCHING POSTS

A scratching post can help keep your cat from scratching on furniture, carpet, or curtains. Many types of posts are available at pet supply stores. You can also make your own scratching post by attaching carpet or **sisal** rope to a wooden post.

sisal—a strong white fiber made from an agave plant

FACT: Some cat play towers come with built-in scratching posts.

NAIL CARE

Birman cats need their nails trimmed every few weeks. Regular trims help reduce damage if Birmans scratch carpet or furniture. Nail trimming also helps protect Birmans from paw injuries and infections caused by ingrown nails.

You can find nail clippers for cats at pet supply stores. These clippers are easy to use and reduce the risk of injury to your cat.

Owners should start trimming their Birmans' nails when the cats are young. Kittens will then become used to having their nails trimmed as they grow older.

DENTAL CARE

Birman cats need regular dental care to protect their teeth and gums from decay. You should brush your Birman's teeth at least once each week. You can use a soft cloth or a toothbrush. Be sure to use toothpaste made for cats. Toothpaste made for people can make cats sick.

GROOMING

Birmans' coats are easier to care for than coats of other longhaired breeds. But Birmans should still be brushed weekly. A natural bristle brush is best to use. A comb works well on thick areas of the coat. You will need to brush your Birman more often in spring when its winter coat is shedding.

Some owners bathe their Birmans occasionally. Bathing can help remove loose hair and keep the cats' coats clean. If you bathe your cat, use a shampoo made for cats.

After cats become used to having their nails trimmed, they usually will sit quietly for trims.

HEALTH CARE

Cats need regular visits to a veterinarian. Most vets recommend yearly checkups. Older cats may need to visit a vet more often. At a checkup, a vet will check your cat for signs of health problems. The vet will also give your cat any necessary **vaccinations**.

Birman cats generally have few health problems. The most common problem is **hairballs**. Many longhaired cats have hairballs at some time in their lives. Large hairballs can become trapped in a cat's digestive system. A vet may have to remove these hairballs.

Regular brushing is the best way to prevent hairballs in Birmans. Brushing removes loose fur before cats can swallow it.

Cats sometimes inherit diseases such as cardiomyopathy from their parents. Cardiomyopathy is a serious heart disease. Responsible cat breeders test their animals for inherited diseases. They will not breed animals that can pass along serious illnesses. But if your cat does develop an inherited disease, your vet can identify and treat it.

vaccination—a shot of medicine that protects animals from a disease

hairball—a ball of fur that lodges in a cat's stomach

Veterinarians use stethoscopes to listen to the sounds of a cat's heart and lungs.

With a look and personality all their own, Birmans stand out in the cat world. With good care, you can help your unique feline friend live a healthy, happy life.

GLOSSARY

breed (BREED)—a certain kind of animal within an animal group; breed also means to mate and raise a certain kind of animal

colorpoint (KUHL-ur-point)—a pattern in which the ears, face, tail, and legs are darker than the base color

crossbreed (kros-BREED)—to mix one breed with another breed

gene (JEEN)—a part of every cell that carries physical and behavioral information passed from parents to their offspring

hairball (HAIR-bawl)—a ball of fur that lodges in a cat's stomach

inherit (in-HAIR-it)—to receive a characteristic from parents

mat (MAT)—to form into a tangled mass

registry (REH-juh-stree)—an organization that keeps track of the ancestry for cats of a certain breed

ruff (RUHF)—long hairs growing around an animal's neck

sisal (SI-suhl)—a strong white fiber made from an agave plant

soul (SOLE)—the spiritual part of a person that is often thought to control the ability to think, feel, and act

vaccination (vak-suh-NAY-shun)—a shot of medicine that protects animals from a disease

READ MORE

Mattern, Joanne. *Siamese Cats.* All About Cats. Mankato, Minn.: Capstone Press, 2011.

Rau, Dana Meachen. *Top 10 Cats for Kids.* Top Pets for Kids With American Humane. Berkeley Heights, N.J.: Enslow Elementary, 2009.

Wilsdon, Christina. *Cats.* Amazing Animals. Pleasantville, N.Y.: Gareth Stevens Pub., 2009.

INTERNET SITES

FactHound offers a safe, fun way to find Internet sites related to this book. All of the sites on FactHound have been researched by our staff.

Here's all you do:

Visit *www.facthound.com*

Type in this code: 9781429666299

Check out projects, games and lots more at
www.capstonekids.com

INDEX